Protecting Your Greatest Asset: Your Mind

Merica Cox

JER 8:22
BALM OF GILEAD
WORLD MINISTRIES

Published by

CGW

2010

Protecting Your Greatest Asset: Your Mind

First Edition February 2010

ISBN 978-0-9565358-0-1

© Merica Cox 2009-2010

Published by:

CGW Publishing
B 1502
PO Box 15113
Birmingham
B2 2NJ

for

Balm of Gilead World Ministries

www.bogministries.org

info@bogministries.org

Foreword by Pastor Ivan Moodley

Merica Cox remains one of the finest of woman preachers to have risen up out of the shores of Africa.

A dynamic and anointed speaker, Merica exposes the Mind and its amazing effect on mankind. Her first book is a must read, not just for the believer but for every individual.

Merica is a minister with diverse giftings and gracings, she writes openly on a subject uncommon to man. A successful church planter, with an Apostolic prophetic mantle, she leaves an indelible mark in the hearts of her hearers.

This book was birthed in the most challenging of seasons while putting in hours studying, pastoring a growing church, overseeing another branch in London and the work in Zimbabwe, engrossed in her circular work, a wife, mother and leader, she remains an amazing success story.

Our greatest struggles are in the Mind and this book attempts to give its readers a better understanding of the Mind and how we could handle this war.

This book is a must read!

Pastor Ivan Moodley

Senior Pastor, Portshepstone Celebration Centre

Durban, South Africa

Dedication

This book is dedicated to my family who have had to pay the price for my being in the ministry

To all those soldiers of the cross of Jesus Christ out there who are laying their lives down for the Kingdom of God

To all the young people who are zealous to get into the battle field. May you fight a good fight of faith armed with the word of truth and trained in the skills of battle.

To all those friends, who have stood by me and supported me in the ministry.

To God Be the Glory For Ever and Ever Amen.

2 Timothy 2:3-5

Endure suffering along with me, as a good soldier of Christ Jesus.

As Christ's soldier, do not let yourself become tied up in the affairs of this life, for then you cannot satisfy the one who has enlisted you in his army.

Follow the Lord's rules for doing his work, just as an athlete either follows the rules or is disqualified and wins no prize.

Merica Cox

A Soldier's Handbook

For these last days

Contents

JER 8:22
BALM OF GILEAD
WORLD MINISTRIES

Is there no Balm in Gilead, is there no physician there? Why then is not the health of the daughter of my people recovered?

Jeremiah 8:22

Preface

In the beginning God said, "Let us make man in our own image, after our own likeness and let them rule over everything we have created"

The question is, which part of a human being is made in the image of God, some scholars feel that our reason, creativity, speech, or self-determination is the image or nature of God. I go along with this line of thinking as it is confirmed in the way that Satan in the garden when plotting the fall of man focused on the reasoning (mind). Man was created an intellectual being and very creative which is God's nature.

Genesis 3:1-7 tells us the story of how Satan negotiated with Eve or shall we say reasoned with her. Many people today fail to accept the Bible as the word of God or even that there is a God because of their reasoning. Thus God himself says "Come let us reason together".

Myles Munroe in his book 'Rediscovering the kingdom' says, "the heart of understanding is precepts and concepts, error is a product of and a result of what is called 'misconception' or 'misunderstanding' the concept of the other person". Satan confused Eve's mind by causing her to question her understanding of what God had said (concept) and making Eve understand

Satan's own concept. "Did God really say?" was the question used by Satan to bring doubt to Eve's mind. Satan knew that if man misunderstood God, man would sin against God and soon drift away in rebellion against God's will which is exactly what Satan and his angels had done. Miles Munroe also said in one of his sermons that when you base your conclusions on wrong assumptions, you will end up with wrong conclusions.

Satan has not changed his strategy; Matthew records how Satan tempted Jesus in the wilderness, "If you are the son of God" Satan said. This is certainly not different from saying "did God really say?", it is all challenging one's mind as to understanding God's precepts and concepts. It opens a door to reasoning's so that Satan can then give you the answers to your questions after you have doubted what you knew to be the truth in the first place.

Why does Satan go to such lengths? Because he wants to exchange the truth for a lie. If you believe a lie you will live a lie and never fulfil your potential. In other words, you will have the wrong vision and spend your life chasing the wrong dream and wondering why happiness and joy always seem to elude you.

How did Jesus deal with Satan during the temptation in the wilderness? Jesus used the word of God. He chose to stand on the word of God rather than believe the lies which Satan was trying to use to seduce him into sinning against God. This is why Paul teaches us to renew our minds so that the same mind that was in Christ Jesus can be also in us. We are exhorted not to be tossed to and fro by every wind of doctrine. This means being established in our minds in the word of God and refusing to be seduced by other concepts that are out there.

The battle for the mind is still going on today. Satan uses everything he can find to confuse, weaken and eventually destroy our minds. Don't give him your mind - stand up and fight. In Ephesians chapter 6, Paul encourages believers to be strong with the Lord's mighty power, putting on the whole amour of God so that you will be able to stand firm against all strategies and tricks of the Devil.

The Devil is a strategist; the Bible says he is like a roaring lion seeking whom he may devour. It is therefore important if we are going to defeat him at his game that we realise that our fight is not against flesh and blood (human beings) but against evil rulers and authorities of the unseen world, against those mighty powers of darkness who rule this world, and against wicked spirits in Heavenly realms.

Satan's best weapon is making people believe that he does not exist, this way he manipulates and destroys them. Sadly they don't even understand what's going on or what is happening to them.

The Lord however has not left us at the mercy of Satan and his demons, he is raising us into an army that will destroy Satan's prisons and let the captives go free. We are not fighting alone, Jesus fights alongside with us. This is illustrated beautifully in the story of Joshua and the walls of Jericho.

Joshua 5:13-15, *As Joshua approached the city of Jericho, he looked and saw a man facing him with sword in hand. Joshua went up to him and asked, 'Are you a friend or foe?' 'Neither one', he replied, 'I am commander of the Lord's army.' At this Joshua answered, 'I am at your command, what do you want your servant to do?'"*

David wrote in Psalm 124, "*Our soul is escaped as a bird out of the snare of the fowlers, the snare is broken and we are escaped, our help is in the name of our Lord who made Heaven and Earth*".

Introduction

Doctors say that when a person's brain dies, the person is considered dead even though the heart may still be beating. The mind makes you who you are; your future depends on how well your mind functions. Your quality of life also depends on your ability to think and reason and to make good judgements and plans.

The mind is also called the soul of a man and this is where your emotions, feelings and mental processes take place. A human being is made up of three parts, the mind (soul), spirit and body. The mind controls all the body functions and emotions while the spirit is the 'religious' part of the person (the real person). You are therefore a spirit, you have a soul (mind) and you live in a body. Every human being feels the urge to worship something, even the atheist believes in the Earth.

Have you ever wondered why there are so many religions in the world, why does man feel the need to worship something? The reason is that when God created man, he breathed his spirit into Adam and Adam became a living soul. This spirit therefore is always looking for God who put it there. When a person dies, the flesh returns to the dust where it came from including the mind (brain) but the spirit returns to God who gave it. Without the spirit the mind too can not live. If therefore your mind and flesh work together they will control the spirit and bring death to it, but if your mind and spirit work together, they will bring the flesh under control and you become alive in God. When you become alive the way God designed you to be then you will fulfil your destiny and find happiness and contentedness. Your spiritual health will eventually determine your physical health. It is vital that you have a healthy mind if you are to enjoy life and achieve your dreams.

Paul tells us in Ephesians that we need to prepare to fight a good fight of faith. Soldiers in real life prepare not only their physical bodies for battle but also their minds. The mind is so powerful that even God acknowledged when man began building the Tower of Babel in Genesis 11. "*God said 'look what man can do when he puts his mind to it, let us go down and stop them'.*"

Look at a man like Martin Luther King who had a dream that affected a whole world. Why is Nelson Mandela such a respected man? Mandela understood that the white man (flesh and blood) was not his enemy but the system he used was. Mandela fought to change the system and the minds of the people who believed in that system so they could see how evil their system was.

Martin Luther King fought the system not the people.

We know these men as people with great minds who achieved great things to change the course of history and nations.

God says; I am building a people of power, I am making a people of praise that will move through this land by my spirit and will glorify my precious name. Truly, creation groans with expectation; to see the sons of God being manifested. Let therefore this mind that was in Christ Jesus be, also in you.

What is the mind?

The Mind is what the Bible calls the "Heart" of a man. Jeremiah 17:9, *"The heart is deceitful above all things"*. King Solomon is well known for his wisdom, for example, in Proverbs 4:23 he says *"Be careful how you think, your life is shaped by your thoughts"*. The heart and mind is a place where our feelings, emotions and thoughts exist.

A person's behaviour is therefore determined by the way they think and understand things. This is why there is a need to transform one's mind to think rightly in order for one to be successful and contented in life.

Ezekiel 11:19, *"And I will give them one heart, and I will put a new spirit within you; and I will take the stony heart out of their flesh, and will give them a heart of flesh."*

As stated above, when we speak of the heart we include the mind which is how we view things which in turn shapes our sense of values. The Bible compares the mind to the eye in Matthew 6:22-23, *"The light of the body is the eye: if therefore thy eye be single, thy whole body will be full of light.*

But if thy eye be evil, thy whole body will be full of darkness. If therefore the light that is in thee is darkness, how great is that darkness!"

The heart also includes our "will" which is the power and freedom to make choices, God has not left us to make choices based on ignorance but has given us all the information we need to make informed choices. The world we live in is about making daily choices, we are responsible for the choices which we make, and this is why we shall give an account before God one day because we have the Bible to guide us and the Holy Spirit. Jesus said those who are led by my spirit are my sons and daughters. The heart also includes our feelings or emotions which are mainly based on how we respond to events which happen in our lives or our loved ones, whether good or bad.

Remember that you have a "body", "soul" and "spirit". The "soul" which is the heart or mind is the focal point of any human being. It is the part which balances the scales of life; this is why someone wrote the song, "It is well with my soul". If it is well with your soul it shall be well also with your body and spirit.

Human beings are always searching for self gratification, and it is believed by some writers that man's main need is that of self esteem (feeling good about oneself). Abraham Maslow in his 'hierarchy of needs' theory states that self actualisation is the highest goal of every human being; before this need is met however the lower needs must first be met, such as:

Physiological needs, which are hunger, thirst, sex and shelter which are basic to ensuring survival.

Safety and Security needs, our desire for stability in order to focus our attention on other areas of life.

Mastery needs, control over things and people and control over one's own affairs.

Acceptance needs, to give and receive love and affection, to have friends and to belong.

Self-esteem needs, to build up our sense of personal worth and to receive respect from others.

Self-actualisation or fulfilment, our need to develop to our full potential, to feel we are contributing something worthwhile.

This quest for happiness or fulfilment is processed in the mind. The world of advertising uses this principle to lure people into temporal happiness and to keep them going round in circles while they make money out of their confusion.

Today, the world moulds our thinking and sets our goals for us and shapes us according to its image; for example the 'size zero' which has made many young people fall into all kinds of evils as they strive to achieve this world image. If you allow the world to fit you into its mould, you will soon be dissatisfied with who you are and eventually you will be confused as to who you are and what your purpose in life is all about.

I look at the life of Michael Jackson with amazement, how he tried so hard to change who he was to such an extent that there is nothing of the real Michael Jackson left on the outside and yet inside he never changed and he does not seem to have found happiness or fulfilment either.

Matthew 6:21 tells us this about what we might find in a person's mind, *"Where your treasure is there your heart will be also"*.

This desire to attain to the worldly standards has led many to pierce their hearts with many sorrows just as Paul warned in 1 Timothy 6:5-12.

"Perverse disputings of men of corrupt minds, and destitute of the truth, supposing gain to be Godliness: from such withdraw thyself. But Godliness with contentment is great gain. For we brought nothing into this world, and it is certain we can carry nothing out.

And having food and raiment, with these let us be content. But they that will be rich fall into temptation, and a snare, and into many foolish and hurtful lusts, which drown men in destruction and perdition.

For the love of money is the root of all evil: which while some have coveted, they have erred from the faith, and pierced themselves through with many sorrows.

But thou, O man of God, flee from these things; and follow after righteousness, Godliness, faith, love, patience, meekness.

Fight the good fight of faith, lay hold on eternal life, to which thou art also called, and hast professed a good profession before many witnesses."

Renewing your mind

Romans 12:2, *Be not Conformed to this world: but be ye Transformed by the Renewing of your Mind, that ye may Prove what is Good, and Acceptable, and Perfect will of God.*

The mind is the battlefield between the powers of darkness and God's plans for your life. There is a battle for your soul and it is a battle that you should take very seriously. Part of the weaponry of the enemy is to make you complacent and uncaring or refuse to believe that there is a battle being waged against you.

Whether you like it or not, whether you believe it or not, the battle goes on with or without your participation. If you do not rise up and fight you will be destroyed. Most Christians like to play dead hoping that the enemy will live them alone, unfortunately this is playing into the hands of the enemy. Do not be a casualty of your own ignorance; God says that his people perish because of lack of knowledge.

Nicky Cruz in his book "Soul Obsession" (page 126) says,

"We have allowed the world to not only affect us but to completely infect us. To take over our hearts and minds and keep us in bondage to sin, even though we convince ourselves that we're free."

Paul, while encouraging the church of the Philippians said, "*Let this mind be in you, which was also in Christ Jesus*" Philippians 2:5.

What was this mind that was in Jesus? Let's look at the life and ministry of Jesus in order to understand what the mind of Christ is.

In Luke 2:49 we see Jesus as a young boy in the temple. His parents had looked everywhere for him and when they found him he said to them, "*How is it that you looked for me everywhere? Did you not know that I must be about my father's business*".

Jesus shows an awareness of his unique relationship to the father as well as a consciousness of his mission. Today the house of God is the last place young people want to be found in. As for Bible study, not many Christians in general attend and this is why most people are ignorant of spiritual matters. Jesus was passionate about the word and the house of God.

The Bible says in the book of Proverbs 29:18, "*Where there is no vision, the people perish or cast of restraint*". The Bible also tells us that the devil uses idle minds. One needs to have a focus in life, Jesus had a focus, and he knew where he was coming from and where he was going. He was the leader and not the led, never allowed peer pressure to divert his attention from what was real to him. Many times we violate our conscience rather than disappoint a friend. The word of God says that you are the head and not the tail; friends should follow you, not the other way around. People followed Jesus everywhere because they said Jesus had "the words of life", what they meant was that he was full of wisdom.

One day as Jesus was going about his business the Pharisees brought a woman before him and demanded that she be stoned according to the Law of Moses for being caught in adultery.

Jesus showed what manner of man he was; he refused to condemn the woman and said "let him who has no sin cast the first stone". Jesus was trying to show them that their system was not fair and while they were busy condemning others, they themselves were not perfect.

If you have a judgemental attitude or blame everyone else for your problems, you will never be satisfied with anything in this life, you will always be finding fault with others and this will bring frustration to your spirit.

Jesus taught that before you can attempt to remove a splinter out of your brother's eye, first take out the log in your own eye so that you can see much more clearly. In other words, don't be too quick to judge others.

Again, we see Jesus at the cross, bleeding, shamed and suffering, yet he looks at the crowd that had yelled "crucify him", the same crowd which had followed him. He had fed and healed their diseases yet they shouted "crucify him". Jesus prays to the Father and says," Father forgive them, for they know not what they do".

So we see that Jesus was full of love and forgiveness, always seeking the good in others.

Paul in Colossians 3:10 speaks to the church and says, *"Put on the new man, who is renewed in knowledge after the image of him that created him"*.

Putting on involves taking off, you can not put on something new without first taking off what you are already wearing. What this means is you need to be willing to empty your mind of your old way of thinking or the way you view things, and allow the word of God to open your understanding, giving you a revelation of a whole new way of life. Paul prays for the church in Ephesus that the eyes of their understanding be opened so that they may know what the hope of their calling is.

James 4:7 says, *"Submit yourselves therefore to God. Resist the Devil and he will flee from you"*.

In Revelation 3:12 Jesus said, *"Him who overcomes will I make a pillar in the temple of my God"*. We need to understand what a pillar stands for. A pillar holds the house together and stops it from falling down during storms or floods. A pillar never moves position, no matter what comes along. You have perhaps seen London Bridge or any other bridge across the rivers or seas, they are held by pillars. Every year you pass over that bridge, it is always where it should be, never changing position.

Years come and go and the bridge is still standing. Heavy vehicles are still passing through until, one day, the pillars are compromised for some reason and the bridge becomes weak and caves in. As it is in the natural, so it is in the spiritual. Jesus likens the people who transform their minds and become like him in thinking to pillars in the temple meaning in the church or in the realm of the spirit.

Becoming a pillar means learning to resist the negative thoughts that come into your mind and threaten to disrupt your life. Paul in Hebrews 12:4 says, *"You have not resisted to bloodshed, striving against sin"*. What is sin? James 4:17, *"To him that knows to do good, and does not do it, to him it is sin"*.

In other words, sin is a violation of your own conscience; the Bible says if your conscience does not condemn you then you have peace with God. Again the Bible says that some have seared their conscience with a hot iron so they can no longer discern sin.

When God created man, he gave him a conscience which is his spirit which is where the laws of God dwell in man. It is through the conscience that man wrestles or reasons with sin; once the conscience has become dull through being always overruled, a person can do shocking things and not see anything wrong with it.

You, as an individual, have a battle to keep a clean conscience which involves fighting off temptation and anything that will defile your conscience so you can remain pure and holy before God. Without holiness you can not and will not see God. God says you must be holy for he is holy.

Peter confirms what Paul said in 1 Peter 5:9, "*Whom resist steadfast in the Faith. Knowing that, everyone else in the world goes through the same*". Paul saw the battle for the renewing of one's mind as a fight, as he writes to Timothy in chapter 6:12 saying, "*So brothers and sisters, fight a good fight of faith, lay hold on eternal life*".

Paul explains to the church in 2 Corinthians 10:4 that the weapons of our warfare are not physical weapons. They are spiritual truths which are strong enough to destroy every lie of the enemy in our minds. Why do we need these spiritual truths?

Paul gives us the answer in his letter to the Ephesians in chapter 6:12. *"Our battle is not against natural elements such as people (flesh and blood), but against authorities and powers, against the world rulers of this darkness, against the spirits of evil in the Heavens."* (BBE). Our battle is spiritual not physical. If you try to fight in the natural you shall fail, but if you can understand the strategy and weapons of the enemy and engage the enemy in the battle ground armed with truth, the word of God, you shall prevail.

The apostle Paul was anxious for Timothy to understand the nature of the war he would have to face and to know the weapons he would need, not only to survive but to overcome. In 1 Timothy 1:18 Paul says, *"This order I give to you Timothy my son, in harmony with the words of the prophets about you, so that by them you may be strong, fighting the good fight."* (BBE)

What was Paul talking about? Paul was actually giving Timothy an order. "Timothy you are a soldier in the army of the Lord, the prophecies spoken over your life confirm this, now you must use the word spoken about your life to fight a good fight".

What does the word of God say about you as a child of God? You are more than a conqueror through Christ who is your strength. You can do all things through Christ Jesus. The battle is not yours but the Lord's, he will fight for you and give you the victory if you stand on his promises.

There are many promises in the word of God for you to fight a good fight with. Maybe you just don't understand what this war is about. What was Timothy going to be fighting?

As you look around you today you can see how the enemy has worked so hard through advertising, television, cinemas etc. to fill people's minds with garbage. Timothy was to always remember, just like Jesus did, that he was a soldier and as such should not waste his time engaging in civilian activities.

A soldier has to watch and always be alert otherwise they would become the casualty in battle.

In Deuteronomy 20:5-9, God gave instructions on how to choose soldiers from amongst the multitudes. These were the disqualifications: if you had built a new house, planted a vineyard, were engaged to be married and if you were fearful and faint hearted you were to return to your house for you were not fit to fight a war.

The question is, why? Because their minds (heart) would not be in the battle, they would be thinking of their private business instead and would be a hindrance and danger to themselves and to others. A soldier must be focused and determined to fight to the bitter end, a soldier can not afford to be fearful but must be strong and courageous. This same method of selection was used in Gideon's army in Judges Chapter 6.

Peter strengthens what Paul is saying in his letter to the church, *"Be serious and keep watch; the evil one, who is against you, goes about like a lion with an open mouth in search for food; do not give way to him but be strong in your faith, in the knowledge that your brothers who are in the world undergo the same troubles"*. 1 Peter 5:8-9

I have heard many preachers saying that this scripture means that the devil is not a lion though he pretends to be one, whereas what Peter is saying is that the devil's tenacity to destroy your life is like that of a hungry lion looking for food.

Now if you know anything about lions then you will realize the seriousness of this scripture. Satan is moving to and fro searching for someone who he can destroy. He will aim for the weak particularly, as they are easy prey. This is why we are encouraged to be strong in the power of Jesus' might.

Remember the story of Job in the Bible, when the sons of God stood before God, Satan was among them. God asked him where he was coming from, and his answer was, *"From walking to and fro the Earth and walking up and down in it."* (Job 1:7) What was Satan looking for?

A young man was brought to our home by a relative after he had gotten himself into trouble with drugs. He had given in to peer pressure and become involved with drugs, and he always thought he was in control and could stop any time he wanted to.

Reality, however, was that he became more and more involved, his use of drugs becoming more and more serious as time went by.

According to him, he started with marijuana then moved to cocaine. At this point he still thought he was in control, as he was now married and had taken on the responsibility of a mortgage, and his life was going well.

One day, after a quarrel with his wife, he decided to go and buy cocaine, and instead he was introduced to crack which is a far stronger drug.

After taking crack he was sick, so a "friend" helped him by showing him another way of using the drug, and it was this drug that shattered his world. He said he would disappear at work during working hours to go and get a fix. His performance at work began to suffer, his marriage broke down and eventually he lost his job. He squandered all his money on drugs and ended up homeless.

I can still hear him sobbing, "I want my life back, I want my family back". I asked why he kept doing it, and his answer was that he had asked himself the same question but every time he tried to stop he would hear a voice at the back of his head telling him he needed a fix. This voice would be so persistent that he would stop what he was doing and go and look for a fix. He said that he could go anywhere, even to a town he had never visited before, and would be able to find drug dealers. He said he could recognise someone who uses drugs and would ask where to get them.

It was at that stage that he began to understand that he was trapped and could not escape.

He had moved in with his drug friends and they lived in one big house. While there he had witnessed things which shocked him, and although he was a drug user he was not a criminal. An argument arose between him and another person in the house and he realised his life was in danger, so he fled.

He had nothing; no money for transport and nowhere to go. When he left his home he had just vanished and his family did not know what had become of him.

He still had a mobile number for one of his relatives and called for help.

He decided he needed help to get out of this dark world he had found himself in, a world of troubled people who used each other to survive yet would kill without a second thought. Each person was only loyal to his or her own need for more drugs.

Satan walks to and fro up and down the Earth hunting for souls, using all kinds of traps to catch his prey. Isaiah 14:17 says that Satan does not open the house of his prisoners.

This young man now realised that his mind was now controlled by this voice that kept pushing him to get more drugs.

The Bible clearly says that to whom you yield your mind you will become enslaved. He clearly hated what he had become but no longer had control over his life; he had become a slave to the desires of the flesh and no longer had self control which is one of the fruits of the spirit.

This young man found himself in the valley of sorrow.

Paul writes to Timothy in his second letter in chapter 2 verse 22, "*Run from anything that stimulates youthful lust, follow anything that makes you want to do right.*"

King David wrote in Psalm 124, *"My soul is escaped out of the snare of the fowler, the snare is broken and I am escaped. My help is in the name of the Lord"*.

Luke 4:18-19: *"Jesus opened the scroll and began to read, 'The Spirit of the Lord is upon me, for he has appointed me to preach Good News to the poor. He has sent me to proclaim that captives will be released, that the blind will see, that the downtrodden will be freed from their oppressors, and that the time of the Lord's favour has come'."*

Jesus was not talking about the financially poor but rather the spiritually poor. You can be a millionaire and be very poor in spiritual matters, thus the valley is full of the rich and poor, the famous and the unknown alike.

Nicky Cruz in his book Soul Obsession (page 137) paints one of the most touching pictures. He says, "The valley is a cold and heartless place to live. It is defined by blindness and drought and hunger.

You can feel rejection, hurt, insecurity, fear and turmoil. You can smell the hopelessness and pain. You can sense anguish and sorrow and the valley has nothing to do with income or social status. It's a state of the heart. It is any place apart from knowing and trusting God"

This is the reason Jesus stepped down from his throne and entered the world of the valley, to live among the hopeless and lost so he could create a bridge between the valley and the mountain top.

There is hope for the captives if they will come to the cross and find Jesus. The name JESUS means; the Lord has become my salvation. Jesus is the saviour of your soul, the ever present help in time of trouble. Only he has the power to set the captive free from bondage. If you call on his name he will hear you and come to your rescue.

The Bible says that whosoever shall call upon the name of the Lord shall be saved. Jesus did not come into the world to condemn the world but that the world through him might be saved.

Why not call on him now and find rest for your soul?

What are our weapons of war fare?

There are four weapons of warfare that we are given in the word of God to fight every form of war, which are illustrated below.

During the days of the prophet Samuel, the people of God were at war with the Philistines. All of Israel was living in fear, even Saul the King was afraid. Young David, on the other hand, was a man who walked with God; he understood the principles of war fare.

The Name of Jesus

In 1 Samuel 7:45, we are told of the events that took place. David said to Goliath, *"You come against me with a sword, and a spear, and a shield: BUT I come against you in the NAME of the Lord of hosts, the God of the armies of Israel whom you defy"*.

A prophet was sent to Zerubabel with this word, *"Not by might nor by power but by my spirit says the Lord"* We are warned not to try to fight in our own strength.

There is power in the name of Jesus. The Bible tells us that the name of the Lord is a strong tower, the righteous run into it and they are saved. John 15:16b, *"That whatsoever you ask the father in my name, he will give it to you"*.

Philippeans 2:9-10, *"Wherefore God also hath highly exalted him, and given him a name which is above every name: That at the name of Jesus every knee should bow, of things in Heaven and things in the Earth, and things under the Earth.*" The Bible says whatever we do, to do it in the name of Jesus.

The word of God (scriptures)

Hebrews 4:12, "*For the word of God is quick and powerful, sharper than any two edged sword*", and David said in Psalm 119:89, "*For ever, O Lord, thy word is settled in Heaven*". The word of God does not change; it will forever perform that which God set it to perform.

Verse 105 says, "*Thy word is a light unto my feet and lamp unto my path*". I don't fight blindly but am led by the word of my God.

Verse 160 says, "*Thy word is true from the beginning: and every one of thy righteous judgements endures for ever*".

The word of God can be trusted to do what God says it will do. Read about the Hebrew boys in the book of Daniel, they are an inspiration of what great faith is like and God's faithfulness to those who dare to trust him.

The blood of Jesus

Revelation 12:11, "*And they overcame the enemy by the blood of the lamb; and the word of their testimony and they loved not their lives unto death*".

There is power in the blood of Jesus, that power is everlasting. Now how can I overcome by the word of my testimony; my testimony gives me confidence in the Lord and helps to boost the level of my faith when faced with a situation which would otherwise defeat me, just like in the story of David and Goliath.

The word of your testimony

My testimony also helps others to build their faith as they hear what God is able to do and as they see me able to stand against all odds they too will believe in my God.

Remember in the book of Daniel, King Nebuchadnezzar declared that everyone should worship the God of Daniel in Babylon because of Daniel's testimony.

A young Christian girl became caught up with sinful behaviour as she engaged herself with worldly friends. She secretly went to parties and learnt to smoke and drink alcohol; she thought she was just pleasing her friends because she did not want them to think she was backward.

Although this began with peer pressure, she inwardly wanted to experiment and see what the other world was like, just in case she was missing out, as many young people do.

1 John 2:15-16, *"Love not the world, neither the things that are in the world. If any man loveth the world, the love of the Father is not in him. For all that is in the world, the lust of the flesh, and the lust of the eyes, and the pride of life, is not from the Father, but is from the world."*

Little did she know that she had opened herself to demon powers from the dark world. She said, "I only did it once", but even if that was true, that was all that the enemy required; just a small compromise and he was in.

Something happened during one of the outings which she could not remember afterwards. She did not return home that night but woke up in a friend's house the next morning. She realised someone must have spiked her drink without her knowing, and she was terrified of what might have happened to her.

A spirit of fear entered her life and she found that she could no longer do the things she used to do because she was now afraid of people. She could not even attend church services any more Her fear became so consuming that she stopped working, stopped attending college and became house bound.

Every time she went somewhere that there were many people, she would suffer panic attacks. These got worse and worse, she lost weight and contact with friends as she felt they saw her as a freak. This went on for three years, at which time she decided to go for counselling and went through the process of repentance, self forgiveness, accepting God's forgiveness and then deliverance.

There is no sin which can not be forgiven, people just have a problem accepting forgiveness and forgiving themselves.

1 John 1:9, *If we confess our sins, he is faithful and just to forgive us our sins, and to cleanse us from all unrighteousness.*

What served this young girl was the fact that she knew the word of God; she repented and would write scriptures and paste them around her room. She felt safe as long as she was in that room. It took three years and a great deal of prayer for her to be able to start living again.

The only good thing that came out of this experience was that her faith as a Christian became much stronger than before as she now understood that there was a real war out there.

Have you heard of the saying, "give the devil a finger and he will take the whole hand?"

This young girl got off very lightly as others can end up raped, diseased, pregnant or even dead.

The only way to beat peer pressure is to know the word of God.

When you know who you are in Christ, you will be the leader not the led, the head not the tail. When you are secure in who you are, your mind is established on the truth of what life is all about. You will no longer see the need to prove a point to anyone or to go with the flow when you should be challenging things.

The Bible says that the righteous are as bold as a lion but as harmless as a dove. Some people may tell you that you have been brainwashed, and in a way this is true because the word of God will cleanse your mind, renew your way of thinking and cause you to see the world from a different perspective.

The power of the mind

Proverbs 23:7, "*For as he thinketh in his heart so is he*". You are or will be the product of your mental conditioning. People can be easily programmed or brain washed as this is commonly known.

Morris Cerullo says in his book One Demon Spirit, "Ever since God created the universe, spiritual powers have had dominion over mental powers; and the powers of the mind have had dominion over the physical realm. Whatever spirits we embrace in our minds will determine what will be manifested in our physical realm".

Paul confirms this in his letter to the Romans in chapter 6:16, "*Do you not know that to whom you present yourselves slaves to obey, you are that ones slaves whom you obey, whether of sin leading to death or of obedience leading to righteousness?*" This is why Paul addresses himself as the slave of Jesus Christ.

The world of the occult has developed many techniques using the power of the mind. They understand that a person can do anything they set their mind to do. The mind has inbuilt mechanisms that enable it to be transformable into any image you want.

When a person is under the influence of drugs for example, they may believe that they can fly and throw themselves down from a tall building to their death. A person's mind can be manipulated into believing almost anything.

Who or what influences your mind controls your life.

Every time you yield control of your mind to someone else, you are opening your spirit to the control of that individual or spirit. Your mind is the doorway to your spirit, and the Bible likens the mind to the eye because it is the entrance to your spirit. This is why you should be careful what you feed your mind with, since it will eventually either liberate you or bring you into bondage. Satan knows this so he designs programs and gadgets to enslave people, and they spend their time and money chasing after the latest invention.

Proverbs 27:20, "*Hell and destruction are never full; so the eyes of man are never satisfied.*"

One day, David, the king of Israel, looked outside and saw a naked woman bathing by the river, he lusted after her even though he knew she was married. When she became pregnant David needed to cover this sin and added murder to his crimes. What you see with your eyes will fill your mind (heart) and your flesh will demanded its fulfilment and like David, you will fall into temptation.

The mind is not only the battleground but it is also a field where seeds can be sewn. Jesus told a parable of the man who sewed good seed in his field, and when the servants went back to the field they were surprised to find that there was also bad seed that had been planted by the enemy.

Paul in Ephesians encourages us to put on the helmet of salvation in order to protect our minds from the seeds that the enemy is throwing our way. Paul encourages believers to work out their own salvation with fear and trembling.

Therefore, you can nurture good seeds and pick out the bad seeds to protect your mind and protect yourself.

Casting down imaginations

John 8:32, *"Ye shall know the truth, and the truth shall make you free"*. Many people including professing Christians are oppressed in their minds; depression is only the one sign that shows something is wrong. When we become emotionally oppressed we find it difficult to deal with little things that go wrong in our lives.

Paul, when writing to the Corinthians, says that we have weapons for pulling down strongholds. You can not pull down a stronghold if you don't know what it is. Most of us have heard of or know someone who has a phobia, but where do phobias come from? The mind is a very delicate and complicated part of our anatomy.

Anxiety, fear, evil imaginations, negative thinking, low self esteem, pride and unbelief, these are the strongholds we need to guard our minds from. Proverbs 6:16-19 tells us of six things which are hated by the Lord. Two of those six things are: a heart full of wicked imaginations and eyes of pride. Proverbs 12:5 also tells us that the thoughts of the righteous are right.

Anxiety is the one negative force that cuts through all levels of society affecting the rich and poor, young and old alike. Anxieties and tensions are insidious forces which exist below the surface of your awareness, smouldering and building up, until you reach a "breaking point" and explode in a fit of anger or a violent argument, or some other unreasoned behaviour.

It also manifests in over-indulgence in food, alcohol, cigarettes, sex or work, in headaches, fatigue, impotence, clumsiness, sleepless nights, or any number of physical ailments.

Conscious worry and fear also enter the picture to compound the feeling of frustration already being experienced because you are not able to identify the source of the unconscious anxiety and thus eliminate it. To add to this state of tension is the sense of "alienation" that modern society produces.

A sense of isolation, separation, powerlessness, pessimism, loneliness, apathy, uninvolvement, meaninglessness, rootlessness, and lack of authentic values.

Alienation may be described as that state in which the individual feels dislocated from himself, from others, from the world in general. Thus it is that man drifts aimlessly through a world seemingly without meaning or purpose - a world he created but over which he no longer exercises conscious control or power.

Man today has lost his identity and his purpose for existing.

Fear

Fear is the primary cause of distorted thinking resulting in inappropriate emotions. Fear is the underlying cause of nightmares and phobias.

Paul writes in his 2nd letter to Timothy in chapter 1:7, *"God has not given us the spirit of fear; but of power and of love, and of a sound mind"*.

Fear is the opposite of faith, because when you believe a lie you will walk in fear but the truth shall make you free. As you can see, fear is a spirit, this spirit makes you see things that are not there or distorts the way things really are.

The spirit of fear will twist everything and make you believe a lie. A sound mind is able to deal with these fears by casting them down.

Fear is the mind killer; the opposite to fear is LOVE. Everything the mind fears is caused by misunderstanding which confuses the mind. Confusion is a state which is uncomfortable and unbearable to the whole body. Unrest in the mind and body causes stress and instability to the spirit.

Remember you are a spirit, you have a mind (soul) and you live in a body. Under this irritation and pain, the natural reaction is to do anything to change the state of confusion. There is a saying that humans fear what they don't understand and destroy what they can't control.

The main cause of possession is lack of love for one's self and the understanding of others within the environment lived in. If a person does not love themselves, it is impossible for them to rationally believe that anyone can love them. This affects how a person perceives themselves and how they believe others perceive them. This is where the imaginations can become the adversary, creating thoughts of low self worth and, in time, the person feels separated from the divine will of God, their family, the community and the world at large.

Because of this isolation, many take their own lives.

Feelings of alienation become the dominant emotion and, if unchecked, this stress then leads to depression. The sufferer can lose the will to live, and the confusion of the mind will cause the unconscious self destruction of the body so as to end all pain and suffering. A person can put themselves in such an unbearable position that they feel there is no more hope.

We are told by scientific researchers that the brain processes an average of 27,000 continuous thoughts a day, and a healthy mind has to balance positive and negative emotions to keep the natural flow of the body's chemistry throughout the highs and lows of everyday life.

The mind may be oppressed due to obsession, and this happens when the brain processes replay the same thought repeatedly, causing it to echo throughout the 27,000 thoughts a day. The echo creates a dominant thought which clouds the mind, leaving no room for new thoughts. This is the main cause of selfishness and self consciousness. A person becomes obsessed with their own self, their own needs, desires and wishes; they have no more mental capacity to think about anyone or anything that does not fulfil these wants. This is what the Bible calls a carnal mind which will bring death.

All the great saints had to overcome their natural instincts which draw one to self centeredness in order to become selfless. They urged their followers to do the same in order to reap the benefits of spirituality.

Imaginations

2 Corinthians 10:5, "*Casting down imaginations, and every high thing that exalteth itself against the knowledge of God, and bringing into captivity every thought to the obedience of Christ*".

When an emotion is felt by the spiritual part of the person, the mind forms an internal picture of what the person is feeling. The picture helps the person to better understand what they are feeling and the reasons why they feel that way and, based on this, they decide what action to take.

When the mind perceives these images, it can not tell the difference between reality and imagination and it then communicates with the spirit, causing it to react with emotional responses.

These imaginations in the mind create the emotions (fear or worry) that one experiences. Imaginations can only disappear when we obey the word and do what it says. The psychologists also use the same technique; they always try to get you to face your fears. Usually, when you have faced them and realised that nothing has happened to you, you are more than willing to face them again. The more you face them, the less hold they have on you.

The question is, why? Your thinking on the issue changes every time you deal with it, your renewed mind begins to gain control as fear is being driven out. Paul calls this "Putting an end to reasonings, and every high thing which is lifted up against the knowledge of God". 2 Corinthians 10:5.

We are warned in Romans 8:6 that if we are carnally minded we shall die but if we are spiritually minded we shall live a good, peaceful life. If you can believe what the word of God says about you, about your fears, your reasonings and your abilities, you can be free from oppression.

How can one achieve this? Philippians 4:8 gives us the answer, where Paul said, *"Finally, brethren, whatsoever things are true, whatsoever things are honest, whatsoever things are just, whatsoever things are pure, whatsoever things are of good report: if there be any virtue, and if there be any praise, think on those things"*.

One has to take care what they feed their minds with, you will eventually become whatever you fill your mind with.

Guilt

Guilt is usually the base of most fears; fear has to do with punishment. Proverbs 23:7, "*As the thoughts of his heart are, so is he*". This is the reason why there is a need for repentance if one is to be free from oppressive thoughts which lead to depression and sometimes suicide.

Confession is necessary to deal with guilt and to facilitate the healing process. James speaks of this in chapter 5:16 of his letter to the church, "*Confess your sins one to another, and pray one for another, that ye may be healed*". There is a proverb which says, "The guilty flee when no one pursues them"

The devil thrives on secrets and unconfessed sins. He uses these to bring guilt into your spirit. Guilt then hinders your prayer life and you begin to withdraw slowly from the presence of God as you now feel unworthy. Your guilt cuts you off from God's presence. This leaves you vulnerable and exactly where Satan wants you. Satan is the enemy of your soul; he wants to destroy you.

Guilt will cause you to doubt God's love, forgiveness, and eventually the word of God. When you are now in the state of unbelief he moves in for the kill, just like a hungry lion.

There are many people with mental health problems who were once active and full of life, and people wonder what went wrong. However not everyone with a mental health problem fits this description. Sometimes there is a medical explanation to the problem which can be corrected through medical intervention.

God is not against doctors and medicine. On the contrary, all knowledge comes from God. God, however, will work even after man has tried and failed.

The computer; an example of the mind

Have you ever wondered why some people never seem to get any healing or deliverance despite all the prayers and laying on of hands over their lives. Well I have, I have prayed for some people, ministered deliverance until I did not know what else to do with the person because nothing seemed to change.

I began to question God about this; I wondered where I was failing because I know God never fails. I soon got to realise what was wrong, it was not God or even me. Sometimes it is not deliverance or healing that is needed but the renewing of the mind.

The mind is the control room, and works just like a computer. The computer will work perfectly until a virus infects it and corrupts its files. The computer needs to be protected from these viruses through the programs designed for that purpose.

The computer virus operates just like the demons do; the devil is the hacker and sends his demons in disguise. The viruses are transferred through files or emails, and unsuspecting people get caught when they open an infected file and the virus then spreads quickly to other files. These files are usually disguised as adverts or information you need to know about.

Usually when your computer has a virus you can spread it to all your friends or business acquaintances when you communicate with them. This is why the Bible says the Devil is like a roaring lion seeking whom he may devour. He designs products that entice people, for example the phonograph.

People often want to try something new or experiment, that's what makes their life exciting, but they unfortunately end up trapped and can't find a way out. This leads to the oppression of their minds. In the same way, people have been trapped in alcoholism, smoking, sexual immorality and drug addiction.

These problems can lead to mental health issues and demonic oppression of the mind, thus producing the paedophiles and sex crimes that so sadly lead to the disappearance of young children as they are either murdered or sold as sex slaves. This is perversion in its highest form, when someone is no longer satisfied with normal sex but is searching for more fulfilment which is never possible or even realistic.

At this stage, the mind is no longer reasoning but is pushed by the spirit of lust which is unquenchable. This is when a person is classified as demented, having lost all self control and sound mind, and this is a frightening place to find yourself in. This is a soul totally lost and in the pits of hell. People who have been on drugs will tell you they have been to hell and back, and this is a good description of what it's all about.

What is oppression? There is a difference between being possessed of the devil and being oppressed of the devil. If a person is possessed, they need to be delivered and then to renew their mind, but if a person is oppressed, it is only their mind that needs renewing according to the word of God.

If a person fails to deal with their oppression, they will eventually become possessed of the devil; their state becomes very difficult to resolve due to their state of mind, and this is why Jesus said, *"This kind goeth not except by fasting and prayer."* in Matthew 17:21.

In the same way, if you do not take heed of the warnings in your computer about virus infection, your computer will slow down and eventually come to a stand still. Paul encourages us in Ephesians 6 to put on the helmet of salvation to protect our minds from the fiery darts of the enemy.

Satan, from the very beginning in the garden, knew where to attack mankind. He did not put sickness or disease on them, he simply attacked their minds and caused them to be confused about what God's instructions were. Confusion brings doubt and doubt brings disobedience and disobedience brings death.

Because man was now cut off from the source of life and well being, it became easy to simply accept whatever the enemy was dishing out, and sickness and disease therefore came as a result of disobedience. Jesus redeemed mankind from this death trap; he took back the keys of the kingdom which Satan had stolen from Adam and gave the keys to the Church which is his body.

Just like the computer, God designed man with a conscience, and this is your anti virus protection unit. Every time a virus (wrong thought) enters your mind, your conscience gives you a warning for you to quickly delete the thought so it does not get a chance to spread and poison the whole system.

The Holy Spirit is the power that deals with the virus and destroys it so there is no trace or effect from it. Your computer is not safe without anti virus protection, as you surf on the Internet you can pick up viruses. In the same way your life is not complete without God's presence and you are not safe from the devices of Satan.

The mind must be guarded against evil thoughts at all times; one negative thought that is allowed to get into the heart will multiply, just like seed which, when planted on fertile ground, will yield a great harvest.

The mind is like a field and thoughts are like seed and, whether good or bad, they will grow and multiply if not plucked out in time. Negative thoughts, like weeds, are destructive in nature and will destroy the positive thoughts leaving you empty and in a valley of sorrow, as explained by Nicky Cruz.

You can nurture your positive thoughts and reap a healthy and abundant harvest.

The keys of the kingdom

Matthew 16:19, *"And I will give you the keys of the kingdom of Heaven: and whatsoever thou shalt loose on Earth shall be loosed in Heaven."*

Keys are a symbol of authority. Jesus here gave mankind the authority which God had given to man before the fall. Genesis 1:26, *"And God said; let us make man in our image, after our likeness: and let them have dominion over the fish of the sea, and over the fowl of the air, and over the cattle, and over all the Earth, and over every creeping thing that creepeth upon the Earth."*

This authority was lost in the Garden of Eden. Jesus, through his death, overcame the enemy and took back that authority and gave it back to man. Colossians 2:15, *"And having spoiled principalities and power, he made a shew or them openly, triumphing over them in it"*.

Satan, however, is not a good loser, so the fight for authority still continues. Satan wants to bring man to his knees, to bow down before him and worship him and not God.

Satan therefore attacks the mind by sowing seeds of doubt and unbelief, confusion and eventually mental breakdown. A confused man can not exercise his authority and a double minded man is unstable in all his ways.

This therefore is the basis for our authority, Matthew 28:18, *"And Jesus came and spoke to them, saying, All power is given to me in Heaven and on Earth, go ye therefore"*.

Jesus transferred this power to us. He gave us a legal right to use it and Satan knows this. In the real world, someone with mental health issues can not be enlisted in the army.

If someone has a mental breakdown while on duty they will be discharged from duty for treatment. If all fails; they will be discharged from the army completely. Can you see this in the spirit? If a quarter of Jesus' army is disqualified or discharged from duty, Satan rejoices. Therefore it is important to maintain a sound mind at all times so we can fight a good fight of faith.

Do you know that we have been made joint heirs with Christ? Romans 8:17, *"And if children, then heirs of God, and joint heirs with Christ; if so be that we suffer with him, that we may be also glorified together."*

In Ephesians 2:6, we are told that God has raised us up together, and made us sit together in Heavenly places in Christ Jesus. Jesus is seated on the right hand of God, which is a place of honour, power, favour and exaltation. Now, if we are seated with Christ in that position of power in the spirit realm, this makes us very powerful indeed.

Luke 9:1, *"Then he called his twelve disciples together and gave them power and authority over all devils, and to cure diseases."*

Luke 10:17-20, *"And the seventy returned with joy, saying, Lord, even the demons are subject to us through thy name. And he said to them, I beheld Satan as lightning fall from Heaven. Behold, I give to you power to tread on serpents and scorpions, and over all the power of the enemy: and nothing shall by any means hurt you. Notwithstanding in this rejoice not, that the spirits are subject to you; but rather rejoice, because your names are written in Heaven."*

John 14:12, *"Jesus said, 'Verily, Verily I say unto you, He that believeth on me, the works I do shall he do also; and greater works than these shall he do; because I go to my father'."*

So I can truly say that I can do all things through Christ who is my strength, and for this reason I must put on the whole amour according to Ephesians 6 in order to protect myself from the attacks of the enemy.

God has given us the weapons and the power to fight the enemy, He has given us the word of truth to use as an anti virus program to automatically detect, delete and clean up all infections or Satanic programs in our minds so that we can run as he intended us to. Should you choose not to use this word, then you will pay the price sooner or later.

The mind is a wonderful thing which certainly needs to be protected. Is yours protected?

Conclusion

Psalm 124, *"Our soul is escaped as a bird out of the snare of the fowlers, the snare is broken and we are escaped our help is in the name of our Lord who made heaven and earth"*.

Your mind is your most valuable asset. You can do without your eyes, legs or hands but you can not function without your mind. Your mind makes you who you are; it shapes your character, your lifestyle and your very being. Your dreams give you hope for tomorrow without which you will wither away in hopelessness and depression. Your mind determines your outlook on life, the way you respond to situations and the way you will deal with pressure, failure and success.

Your mind is alive, therefore it needs to be fed. What you feed your mind with will determine your lifestyle and therefore your future and destiny. If your mind is healthy you will be a productive member of society, but if your mind becomes infected by satanic viruses you could become the next paedophile, Jack the Ripper, homeless person, thief, murderer, drug addict, alcoholic or suicide victim.

The Bible encourages parents to train their children while still young in the way they should go and when they are older they will not depart

---

from that which has been embedded in their minds.

The mind has great capacity to learn and unlearn, and this is why you can delete from your mind some of the negative things which might have found their way in. You can use the word of God as an antivirus to wash away the negative stuff which you have picked up along the way. The Bible calls this experience "repentance from dead works" or transformation.

If your mind is so important for your very existence, don't you think it deserves your best attention? People look after their hearts, eyes, muscles, skin and so on but forget that it does not matter how strong your heart is, if your mind is dead, you are dead. The only good your heart will do is to be donated to someone with a live mind and a dead heart so they can continue to live.

You may be breathing, you may be sitting at your desk, you may be watching TV but you might also know what it feels like to be dead in your mind. When someone is in a job that they don't enjoy, that demoralises them, they say that they are performing 'mindless tasks', and that is a waste of the greatest asset that they have.

Remember Romans 12:2, "*Be not Conformed to this world: but be ye Transformed by the Renewing of your Mind, that ye may Prove what is Good, and Acceptable, and Perfect will of God.*"

Our greatest struggles are in the mind, and now that you have a better understanding of the mind, its struggles and of spiritual warfare, you can understand how, together, we can fight this war and win.

For those already in a crisis, this book may help them to understand what the problem is and to do something. For those not in a crisis, they can realise these dangers and avoid becoming a victim to them and perhaps be in a better position to help others.

Your mind is so delicate and so very precious, and without it there is no you. There is a thin line between sanity and insanity, and anyone can become a victim.

Fight to keep your mind safe, protect your mind at whatever the cost and remember that prevention is better than cure.

The battle for the mind is still going on today, yet we are not fighting alone; Jesus fights alongside us.

Let us stand together and fight now.

Bibliography

Transforming the Mind

Peter Shepherd

Available online at www.trans4mind.com

Rediscovering the Kingdom - Ancient Hope for Our 21st Century World

Miles Munroe

Destiny Image Publishing, 2004

ISBN-13: 9780768422177

One Demon Spirit

Dr Morris Cerullo

Morris Cerullo World Evangelism, 1993

Soul Obsession: A Passion for the Spirit's Blaze

Nicky Cruz

Hodder & Stoughton, 2005

ISBN-13: 9780340863336

The Balm of Gilead World Ministries

Balm of Gilead World Ministries was started in 1996 by Merica and Joel Cox in Bulawayo, Zimbabwe for the Glory of God.

The family had returned to Zimbabwe from Zambia where they had served as missionaries and the church began in their family home in North End. The first service was attended by 15 people and three months later the meeting+s moved to a college hall in Lobengula Street. The church continued to grow and six months later the meetings moved again to the bigger hall at the Academy of Music.

The name Balm of Gilead comes from Jeremiah chapter 8 verse 22, "Is there no Balm in Gilead, is there no physician there? Why then is not the health of the daughter of my people recovered?

The Balm of Gilead logo came to Merica in a vision which she saw a rainbow, inscribed with the words "What is your hearts desire?". She answered, "To be like Jesus and to do the works which Jesus did, even greater works" and then saw a cloud ascending and lifting the rainbow higher into the sky. Merica chose the rainbow as a reminder of what she felt was a covenant with God, just as God made a covenant with Noah and gave him a rainbow for a sign.

In 2001, Merica came to the United Kingdom and settled in High Wycombe, starting a church in her lounge in Dashwood Avenue. The group later moved to Green Street Community Centre, again to the Reggie Grove Centre and later to the current location at the Wye Valley Community Centre.

In 2005, due to the number of people who were commuting from east London, another branch was opened in Romford, Essex.

In 2006 the Cox family moved to Wellingborough in Northamptonshire where a few months later they started holding services, giving birth to yet another branch.

We thank the Lord for his faithfulness and pray he will use this ministry as a tool in His Hand for His Glory.

You can learn more about the Balm of Gilead World Ministries at our website:

www.bogministries.org

info@bogministries.org

JER 8:22
BALM OF GILEAD
WORLD MINISTRIES

Lightning Source UK Ltd.
Milton Keynes UK
UKOW06f1824260416

273026UK00003B/9/P